Advanced

Rhythm

Theory

*Rhythmic Serialism and Non-Dyadic Time
Signatures*

Dedication:

This work is dedicated to my teachers and

mentors: Ms. Mccombe and Mr. Smith. Thank you

for being an instrumental part in my music

education.

Note to the reader

Dear Reader,

In this book you will learn about rhythmic serialism and non-dyadic time signatures. Since each topic is more advanced and can be, at times seemingly unrelated, each topic is given a dedicated section. Section one covers what serialism is and how rhythmic serialism is similar to and a continuation of pitched serialism by Arnold Schonberg as well as how to approach and use it. However, section two explains non-dyadic time signatures. For this section one must depart from traditional ways of thinking about meters and must instead focus on the bigger picture. Both rhythmic serialism and non-dyadic time signatures alike require practice as both are seldom discussed.

However, when one takes the time to discover, practice and learn these skills their overall musicianship and theory knowledge will benefit. Since these topics are so rarely talked about I took it upon myself to compile them into one book so they may be easily accessed. These things being said, let us begin.

- Will Holmes

Part One: Rhythmic Serialism and

Free time

Abstract

Rhythmic Serialism is the phenomenon in music in which rhythm may be serialized after they are assigned a numerical value from either one to twelve or zero to eleven. This paper explains the meaning behind and the understanding of music in this manner and analyzes and explains the patterns as they occur. Since Schoenberg's work with pitched serialism and his twelve-tone matrix serialized pitch, the rhythmic matrix similarly serializes rhythms. This paper includes hexi rhythmic combinatorial analysis, interpretation and explanation of matrix reading and comprehension and navigation of the matrix, as well as a resolution to free time misalignment.

Introduction to Rhythmic Serialism

In the 1920's Arnold Schoenberg devised a system in which each pitch of an octave can be used equally so that no individual pitch is given importance over another and this concept was later called atonality, as in tonal music some notes such as the tonic, mediant and the dominant, and leading tone(which can be natural or flattened to create either a Major or minor seventh form the root of the chord) which are important and focused sounds. However, Arnold Schoenberg and his colleagues in the 1920s were focused on pitch serialization and only recently have composers, music theorists, and musicians alike focused on other aspects of music that may be serialized in a similar fashion. While the basics of movement are generally agreed upon, more intricate and detailed fastest of Rhythmic Serialism are often ignored, thus this paper aims at focusing on those aspects of Rhythmic Serialism.

<u>Navigation Terminology</u>

Analyzing left to right: The prime row.

Analyzing right to left: The inverse row.

Analyzing top to bottom: The opposite column.

Analyzing bottom to top: The inverse opposite

column.

The
Oppisate
Column
⇩

0	1	2	3	4	5	6	7	8	9	10	11
11	0	1	2	3	4	5	6	7	8	9	10
10	11	0	1	2	3	4	5	6	7	8	9
9	10	11	0	1	2	3	4	5	6	7	8
8	9	10	11	0	1	2	3	4	5	6	7
7	8	9	10	11	0	1	2	3	4	5	6
6	7	8	9	10	11	0	1	2	3	4	5
5	6	7	8	9	10	11	0	1	2	3	4
4	5	6	7	8	9	10	11	0	1	2	3
3	4	5	6	7	8	9	10	11	0	1	2
2	3	4	5	6	7	8	9	10	11	0	1
1	2	3	4	5	6	7	8	9	10	11	0

⇧
The Inverse Oppisate
Column

⇦ The Inverse Row

Rhythmic Serialism Terminology

Hexi Rhythms: Six consecutive rhythms as they appear in the matrix either left to right (or vice versa) or top to bottom (or vice versa).

Matrix Division: Dividing the matrix into four equal quadrants. To make the quadrants one must go a hexa rhythm right from the first number in the first prime row, and also, they must go down a hexa rhythm from that same point and create an "X" and "Y" axis dividing both the left to right rows and the top to bottom columns in half.

Content of Each New Matrix: Upon an initial subdivision the twelve by twelve (12x12) matrix will become a (6x6) matrix. The new matrix (6x6) is composed of tri rhythms (half of a hexi rhythm), which are the first or last three rhythms right or left, and the first or last rhythms going top to bottom. Tri Rhythms, hexi rhythms, and divided matrices are examples of rhythm groups.

<u>The Rules of Matrix Progression</u>

Simple Movement: Moving in one direction on one row or column. (left or right, up or down)

Compound Movement: Moving in one direction on one row or column until there is a shared rhythm on the row either below/above or next to (right or left) of the original row/column that was started. This movement may be done multiple times, provided that the rows change to another row and the columns change to another column. (E.g. column to column, row to row).

Complex Movement: Moving in one direction on one row or column and then changing to the other direction. (E.g. starting on a row and ending on a column). Complex movement occurs one time.

Compound Complex Movement: Moving in one direction on one row or column and then changing to the other direction. (E.g. starting on a row and ending on a column). However, unlike Complex Movement, Compound Complex Movement occurs multiple times similar to Compound Movement. (E.g. column to row to column)

Assigning Rhythms Numerical Values

Rhythms Regarded as Numbers: Gather a collection of twelve notes of different rhythmic values, (E.g. a quarter, sixteenth and thirty second note, etc.) then assign each a numerical value either from zero to eleven or one to twelve (both will yield the same results, they will just appear differently, as one is zero and eleven is twelve). The numbers can also represent small rhythms besides one note, i.e. they could be two eighth notes beamed together. Then arrange the prime row by placing the rhythms, as they are represented in numerical form in any order. Then fill in all other rows/columns by using the same technique as traditional serialism (this time

however, with rhythms).

Beat Totals Across the Matrix

and Free time

Equivalent Movements: Rows are equal to rows in the number of beats going from right to left, or left to right in simple motion (I.e. the Prime Row is equal to the inverse row). Columns are equal to columns moving in simple motion going from the top to the bottom and the bottom to the top. (I.e. the Opposite Column is equal to the Inverse Opposite Column). Additionally, the outsides of the Matrix are equivalent, I.e. the Prime row is equal to the inverse row which is equal to the opposite column which is equal to the inverse opposite column.

Abandonment of Time Signature: Since the different rhythms are to be used to go from one end to another, one must abandon time signatures as the values of the notes will not all fit into one measure of the "standard" time signatures (common time, cut time,3/4,6/8, or 9/8, etc.) This being the case free time (a lack of a time signature) must be used instead.

Free time Misalignment: Due to the difference in the value of the notes as they appear throughout the matrix it is easy for there to be two completely different and unrelated rhythms among different "voices" or parts. The concept where notes are rhythmically unrelated and seemingly "random" is called Free time Misalignment. Free time

Misalignment may cause issues with phrasing, separating sections/periods and may cause conflicts at the end of the piece as a whole (assuming the composer intends to have all parts and/or voices end simultaneously).

Fixing Free time Misalignment: To resolve the issues presented by Free time Misalignment one must use either complex, compound or compound complex movement in order to ensure that the resultant rhythm is either equal or proportional (e.g. two eighth notes against a quarter note or two quarter notes).

Free time Alignment: When rhythms across voices or parts match or are an equal or more traditional ratio or more traditional functional path. (e.g. two

quarter notes against an eighth note).

Advanced Rhythmic Serialism

Techniques

Matrix Super positioning: Since the Rhythmic Matrix as so far described is generally a twelve by twelve grid, it may be overlaid or superimposed onto a twelve-tone matrix. However, upon this, the rules of both Rhythmic Matrices and Pitched Matrices collide and thus both sets of rules/principles must be followed.

The Six by Six Matrix: The six by six matrix is essentially one quadrant of a twelve by twelve rhythmic matrix. In the Six by Six Matrix the rules of motion are the same as they are in a full twelve by twelve matrix, however there are no Hexa

Rhythms and instead there are tri rhythms. Tri Rhythms divide this matrix in half both up and down, and left and right. Additionally, diagonally through the matrix is a common tone.

The Three by Three Matrix: The three by three matrix is essentially half of a six by six matrix and is significantly less than a twelve by twelve matrix. In the three by three matrix the rules of motion are the same as they are in a full twelve by twelve matrix, however there are no Hexa Rhythms and since three is a prime number there is no "half of" a three by three matrix so there is no concept similar to a hexa rhythm. Additionally, diagonally through the matrix is a common tone, just like a normal twelve by twelve matrix and a three by three matrix.

Why Rhythmic Matrices Work

with Free Time

Similar to how the 12-tone technique ensures that no one pitch is given significance over another, with rhythmic serialism, no one rhythm, or note value is given significance over another. Furthermore, since meters require a certain number of beats in a bar (as defined by the time signature) since there are different rhythmic values, you cannot use rhythmic serialism in any meter, unless you use slurs/ties.

Reference Matrix Illustrations

0	1	2	3	4	5	6	7	8	9	10	11
11	0	1	2	3	4	5	6	7	8	9	10
10	11	0	1	2	3	4	5	6	7	8	9
9	10	11	0	1	2	3	4	5	6	7	8
8	9	10	11	0	1	2	3	4	5	6	7
7	8	9	10	11	0	1	2	3	4	5	6
6	7	8	9	10	11	0	1	2	3	4	5
5	6	7	8	9	10	11	0	1	2	3	4
4	5	6	7	8	9	10	11	0	1	2	3
3	4	5	6	7	8	9	10	11	0	1	2
2	3	4	5	6	7	8	9	10	11	0	1
1	2	3	4	5	6	7	8	9	10	11	0

2	5	4	3	9	8	11	7	6	10	0	1
11	2	1	0	6	5	8	4	3	7	9	10
0	3	2	1	7	6	9	5	4	8	10	11
1	4	3	2	8	7	10	6	5	9	11	0
7	10	9	8	2	1	4	0	11	3	5	6
8	11	10	9	3	2	5	1	0	4	6	7
5	8	7	6	0	11	2	10	9	1	3	4
9	0	11	10	4	3	6	2	1	5	7	8
10	1	0	11	5	4	7	3	2	6	8	9
6	9	8	7	1	0	3	11	10	2	4	5
4	7	6	5	11	10	1	9	8	0	2	3
3	6	5	4	10	9	0	8	7	11	1	2

0	4	7	11	2	5	9	1	6	10	3	8
8	0	3	7	10	1	5	9	2	6	11	4
5	9	0	4	7	10	2	6	11	3	8	1
1	5	8	0	3	6	10	2	7	11	4	9
10	2	5	9	0	3	7	11	4	8	1	6
7	11	2	6	9	0	4	8	1	5	10	3
3	7	10	2	5	8	0	4	9	1	6	11
11	3	6	10	1	4	8	0	5	9	2	7
6	10	1	5	8	11	3	7	0	4	9	2
2	6	9	1	4	7	11	3	8	0	5	10
9	1	4	8	11	2	6	10	3	7	0	5
4	8	11	3	6	9	1	5	10	2	7	0

0	1	2	3	4	5	6	7	8	9	10	11
11	0	1	2	3	4	5	6	7	8	9	10
10	11	0	1	2	3	4	5	6	7	8	9
9	10	11	0	1	2	3	4	5	6	7	8
8	9	10	11	0	1	2	3	4	5	6	7
7	8	9	10	11	0	1	2	3	4	5	6
6	7	8	9	10	11	0	1	2	3	4	5
5	6	7	8	9	10	11	0	1	2	3	4
4	5	6	7	8	9	10	11	0	1	2	3
3	4	5	6	7	8	9	10	11	0	1	2
2	3	4	5	6	7	8	9	10	11	0	1
1	2	3	4	5	6	7	8	9	10	11	0

2	5	4	3	9	8	11	7	6	10	0	1
11	2	1	0	6	5	8	4	3	7	9	10
0	3	2	1	7	6	9	5	4	8	10	11
1	4	3	2	8	7	10	6	5	9	11	0
7	10	9	8	2	1	4	0	11	3	5	6
8	11	10	9	3	2	5	1	0	4	6	7
5	8	7	6	0	11	2	10	9	1	3	4
9	0	11	10	4	3	6	2	1	5	7	8
10	1	0	11	5	4	7	3	2	6	8	9
6	9	8	7	1	0	3	11	10	2	4	5
4	7	6	5	11	10	1	9	8	0	2	3
3	6	5	4	10	9	0	8	7	11	1	2

0	4	7	11	2	5	9	1	6	10	3	8
8	0	3	7	10	1	5	9	2	6	11	4
5	9	0	4	7	10	2	6	11	3	8	1
1	5	8	0	3	6	10	2	7	11	4	9
10	2	5	9	0	3	7	11	4	8	1	6
7	11	2	6	9	0	4	8	1	5	10	3
3	7	10	2	5	8	0	4	9	1	6	11
11	3	6	10	1	4	8	0	5	9	2	7
6	10	1	5	8	11	3	7	0	4	9	2
2	6	9	1	4	7	11	3	8	0	5	10
9	1	4	8	11	2	6	10	3	7	0	5
4	8	11	3	6	9	1	5	10	2	7	0

<u>Conclusion of This Section</u>

In conclusion Rhythmic Serialism can be used in more experimental and modern/contemporary music as it, like the twelve-tone technique exemplifies free rhythmic flow, just as the twelve-tone technique exemplifies "free" tonality (atonality). Additionally, overlapping and the combination of serial approaches to rhythm and pitch combined can be used to create more experimental and unique compositions as in the modern era composers are overly indoctrinated in tonal and traditional rhythmic thought. By creating and utilizing systems in which the composer may work against the "pre-established system" in order to create rhythmically interesting and advanced music, as opposed to overly formulaic and older styled music.

Part Two: Non-Dyadic and

Fractional Time Signatures

Time Signatures and Meter

Before diving into more complicated meter and time signature concepts one must first understand a few underlying basic concepts. The first of which is traditional time signatures and meters. Time signatures and meters organize notes and/rests into time, this organization is represented by a fraction called a time signature. The top number of a time signature represents the amount/quantity of beats represented by the bottom number. For example, in 5/4 time there are five (5) quarter notes (¼) whereas 6/8 times represents six eighth notes (per bar/measure). Both 4/4 and 6/8 are common time signatures and 4/4 is so common that it is known as common time and may be represented on a staff as "C". However, both time signatures are structurally different, and to understand this one must understand the difference between simple and compound meters.

Simple Meter

As its name suggests, a simple meter is one of the most basic kinds of meters. Simple meter by definition means that the beat can be divided by two. For example, 4/4 is a simple meter as it (the bottom number) is divisible by two. However, 4/4 and simple meters may be further divided into more specific categories. Common time (4/4) is a type of simple (divisible by two) quadruple meter. This is because common time is four beats (notated by the top number) of quarter notes. While common time (4/4) is a simple quadruple meter what about other simple time signatures? What kind of meter is 3/4? Since common time was a quadruple meter we can assume that 3/4 is a simple triple meter, and if you thought it was a simple triple meter you would be correct. This is because the top number is the "triple component" and the bottom number describes the "simple meter" nature of this time signature. However, what about 6/8 and 9/8?

Compound Meter

While simple meter is defined as benign divisible by two, compound meter is defined as benign divisible by three in the same way in which simple meter is defined. However, for one to make the leap from compound meter to further classifying the meter one must understand the difference between "big" and "little" beats/pulses. For example, 3/4 has one pulse whereas 6/8 has two. To further explain this the counting for 6/8 and 3/4 will be provided. In 3/4 one counts ONE TWO THREE, where the capitalization indicates the big beat, whereas in 6/8 one counts ONE two three FOUR five six or they may count ONE two three TWO three. As can be observed 6/8 is two "groups of three" and this idea of grouping rhythms will be important later on. Since 6/8 has two pulses of three it is a type of duple (two groups/pulses) compound meter (divisible by three).

Time Signature and Meter

Summary

- Time signatures and meters organize notes into a specified period of time.

- Time signatures are represented by a fraction where the top number represents the amount (quality) of beats defined by the bottom number. Such that 4/4 time signifies four (the numerator) quarter notes (the denominator) per bar/measure.

- Simple meters are, by definition, divisible by two whereas compound meters are divisible by three. Therefore 4/4 (common time or "C") is a simple meter and 6/8 is a compound meter.

- Simple and compound meters can be further classified into duple, triple and quadruple simple/compound meters.

Tuplets

Many musicians are familiar with triplets which are a three note tuplets. Tuplets are notes that take the place of another note or notes. For example, an eighth note triplet may take the place of a quarter note. However, tuplets are not limited to triplets nor are they restricted to eight notes. One may write a quarter note quintuplet, which is five quarter notes in the space of another note. This being said, it is important to understand a few major aspects of tuplets. The first thing that should be noted is that tuplets are equal to other types of tuplets according to the already established rules. This means that since a quarter note is equal to two eighths, a quarter note tuplet can be written in eighth notes (two eighth notes per quarter note as was established).

Another major aspect of tuplets is that they may be accented where the accent is intended to be stronger than the notes surrounding it. For example, a three-quarter note triplet may each be accented on the first eighth note, however they may also be accented on the first and third ethanoate and the difference in accent/emphasis creates a different rhythmic feel, thus since the "feel" of the rhythms are different. The first example of three-quarter note triplets where the accent is on the first eighth note of each is counted thus: ONE two three TWO two three THREE two three. The second example with accents on the first and third eighth notes of the triplet is counted thus: ONE two THREE TWO two THREE THREE two THREE.As the tuplet concept progresses further it is critical to take note of the differences in accent and overall difference in feel given by the accents. To exemplify this idea, examples will be provided below.

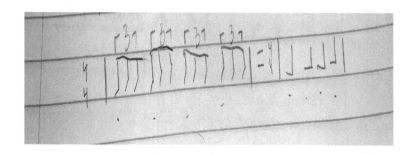

Yet another important thing to consider when approaching tuplets is the value of the notes inside the tuplets bracket. That is to say that quarter note triplets are longer than eighth note triplets and sixteenth note triplets are faster than quarter note triplets. This concept is not foreign however as traditionally sixteenth notes are faster than footnotes, and endnotes are faster than quarter notes. After having understood these ideas regarding tuplets one may ask and desire to see examples so that they may easier visualize these concepts. Therefore, below are examples from famous works. The first example is the introduction from the first movement of Beethoven's "Op. 27 No.2" commonly known as the "Moonlight Sonata".

Tuplets Summary

- Tuplets are multiple notes taking the space of other notes (for example a triplet is equal to (in common time) one quarter note.

- Tuplets are not limited to triplets nor are they limited to eight notes (i.e. quintuplet quarter notes are permissible)

- Tuplets function within traditional rhythmic divisions such that two eighth notes are equal to a quarter note (even in a tuplet).

- Accents may be placed on tuplets and indicate where emphasis should be placed and on what part of the tuplet. (Whether it is a triplet, quintuplet or otherwise).

- Tuplets may exist within other tuplets and this idea is referred to nested/nesting tuplets.

<u>Nested Tuplets</u>

Quintuplets are a combination of two and three therefore could one say that a quintuplet is equal to a duplet and a triplet? Yes, and since this is the case tuplets may be placed inside of other tuplets. Thinking of a quintuplet of eight notes (five eighth notes) instead of beaming them all together, one could beam the first three together (a triplet) and the last two together (a duplet) therefore a triplet and duplet being inside of a quintuplet lay the foundation for expansionary thinking in the realm of nested tuplets. To assist in visualizing this concept an illustrated example will be provided below.

As is the case in tuplets that are not nested, nested tuplets are not limited to quintuplets nor are they limited to triplets and duplets. For example, take a triplet of quarter notes. Since a quarter note is equal to four sixteenth notes, the quarter note triplet may be written as four sixteenth notes. Inside of the quadruplet of sixteenth notes a triplet exists with a remainder of one sixteenth note. Therefore, we can nest a triplet of sixteenth notes inside of a quarter note which is part of a quarter note triplet. One question that may stem from this example may be "what can happen to the remaining sixteenth note? "There are multiple different answers to that question. Such as it may be tied or left alone. Ultimately the choice is the composers.

To help visualize nested tuplets examples will be provided below, as in order to understand non-dyadic and fractional time signatures an understanding of tuplets and nested tuplets is critical.

Examples of Nested Tuplets in Complex Time Signatures

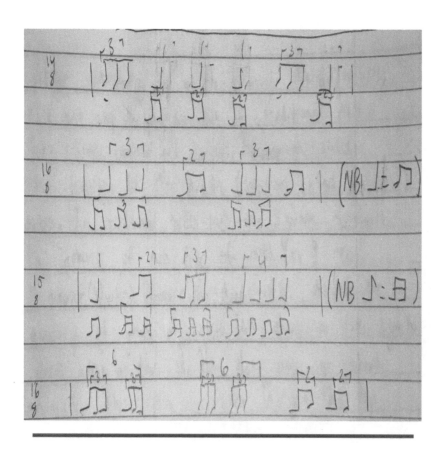

Nested Tuplets Summary

- Tuplets take the value of other notes and likewise nested tuplets take the value of other tuplets values.

- Nested tuplets take the space of part of a larger tuplet.

Non-Dyadic Meters

After understanding all of the previously described concepts, the next step is to discuss and learn about non-dyadic meters otherwise known as irrational meters. In traditional time signatures the number refers to the type of note that gets the beat, whereas in irrational or non-dyadic meters the time signature refers to the quantity of tuplet groups. This means a time signature may appear as thus (3/18). However, how does one go about analyzing and understanding these time signatures? To understand the numerator, one must count the number of tuplet groups and will multiply that number by the value of a complete tuplet group. For example, 4/20 time may have four groups of quintuplets.

It should be observed that a formula may be derived in the case of non-dyadic and/or irrational meters and that formula is $TS = G/ (G \times T)$. That is to say that the Time Signature is equal to the Group (over) the group (of tuplets) multiplied by the Tuplets. Such that (in the example above) $4/20 = 4/ (4 \times 5)$. However non-dyadic meters are not limited in group size or tuplet value (T). Therefore, there are an infinite amount of possible time signatures (TS). Before progressing into fractional non-dyadic time signatures, examples of simpler irrational/ non-dyadic time signatures will be provided.

Non-Dyadic Meter
Examples

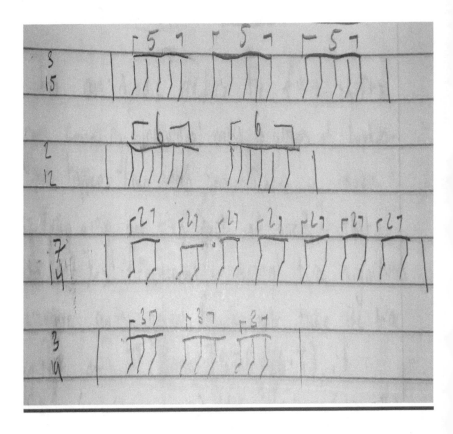

Non-Dyadic Meters Summarized

- Traditional meters focus on the amount of a specified rhythmic value (e.g. 4/4)

- The numerator in a non-dyadic time signature represents the group of tuplets (G). Whereas the denominator represents the groups of tuplets multiplied by the value of tuplets. Therefore, the formula is TS = G / (G x T).

- There is no limit to the quantity of groups, or tuplets in each group, therefore there are an infinite number of possible time signatures.

Fractional Time Signatures

In non-dyadic meters the focus shifts from counting individual notes, to counting groups of tuplets. However, what happens when one only possesses a fraction of a group? The answer is that one would then have a fractional group and therefore the time signatures numerator and denominator would represent this fractional group in their respective manners. Taking the example of 2.5/15, we know that TS = G / (G x T). Therefore 2.5/15 = 2.5 / (2.5 x T). We are left with the question "what times two and a half equals fifteen? The answer is six. Therefore, two and a half sextuplets are in one measure of 2.5/15 (I.E two sextuplets and a triplet are in each measure).

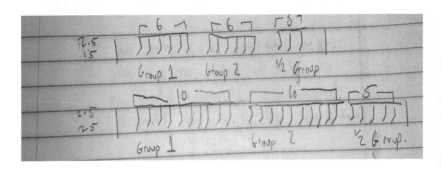

Of course, fractional time signatures are not limited to only halves and may include thirds or other fractions. Keeping in mind that the fraction merely represents part of a group of tuplets and therefore should not be feared. Furthermore, be mindful of each decimal/ fractional time signature as it may imply the need for note values different from the rest of the tuplet group.

Examples of this concept may be seen on the next page.

Fractional Time Signature Examples

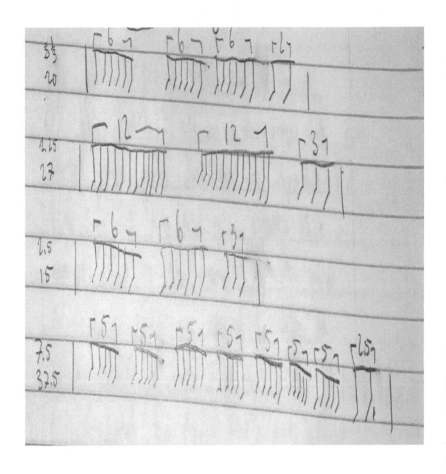

Fractional Time Signature Summary

- Non-Dyadic time signatures count groups of tuplets (TS = G / (G x T)).

- Fractional Non-dyadic time signatures count groups and fractional/partial groups of tuplets.

- In some cases, fractional time signatures may require dotted or otherwise augmented/diminished note values that may be different from other notes in the group/groups.

Conclusion and Final Thoughts

In closing, it is important for musicians to realize why the systems that we use work even at their most basic level. Then we should strive to expand upon them as if we only accepted 4/4 as an example we would have probably never invented the waltz. Ultimately it is the responsibility of every musician to submit their own understandings of the musical world as we continue to learn more and more about what it means to play and listen to music. By no means have I covered all of rhythmic theory, however with understanding of an expansion to serialism and the understanding and internalization of meter, one is in a strong position in the field of rhythm.

May you continue to learn more and may the musical community continue to grow and expand.

Made in United States
Troutdale, OR
06/25/2024

20795702R10037